I Thought the Grass Was Greener

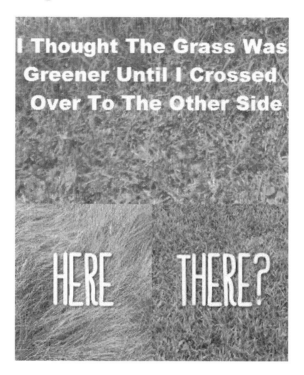

About The Author,

Lakyshia Shelton born September 21 1988, to the parents of Mary and Lorenzo Shelton. She is the youngest of her sibling and a mother of two handsome sons.

Lakyshia was born in Pahokee Fl, but raised in Clewiston Fl.

Lakyshia is the Author of Let's Help Each Other Can You Relate To These Stories, Sex In The Strangest Places, Sex In The Air Let's Get Buck Wild, Poetry Of Life Part 1-3, My Baby Daddy and The Family Drama That Came Along With It, I Thought I Married A Man, A Children's Book To Learn Color Play and Search, Pick Me Color Me coloring book and last but not least It's Coloring With A Twist!

Lakyshia is currently working on more books that are coming soon!

Table of Contents

Prologue:

The Beginning

Dear Diary,

Kerry fresh out of the marriage (but in all reality they were still married) with Jim then ran to Tyrie with open venerable arms. Little did she know that would be a big mistake! When your hurt you shouldn't move to fast and dive into another relationship because you are only going to take that anger out on your new mate, everyone warned Kerry! But no Kerry was very hard headed and only listened to what she wanted. Now you would think that she would've waited longer because after all her husband had done to her, I knew she was moving too fast. See Jim married Kerry only one year prior to the marriage failing. They made the perfect couple and did almost everything together, you could tell that their relationship was strong, but it wasn't strong enough to work through the issues. See before Kerry married Jim she revealed that she cheated on him with an ex and they agreed to work past it. Then over the next year and a half they was having problems because Jim would be on those dating sites, and then he would turn over with a hard dick expecting her to want sex. Then he would be right on her computer in her face looking at and commenting on other chicks pictures, but when a guy even says Kerry picture look beautiful he would snap. Then it really had to be hard after she found out not even one month after they separated that her husband supposed to have two kids on the way and two weeks later another girl was supposed to be pregnant. So in total that made it three babies he was supposedly expecting while they were still married. So now to see my cousin with Tyrie so soon, I knew she was only looking for comfort. What I didn't like was her thinking the grass were greener on the other side, when in reality this guy was not any better because he is doing the exact same thing and Kerry was blinded by the lies he spoke into her ear. Tyrie and Kerry are living life just fine in Lee County Florida in a three bedroom, two baths, one car garage duplex. They have little arguments and fights but for the most part they were in love, and even though Tyrie didn't have anything Kerry still loved him and thought she had something good, until he thought she was stupid. I mean he wanted to get her pregnant, but it was too early and she was still trying to work things out with her husband. The main thought was even though they hurt each other Kerry would have never dreamed that Jim would go as far as to making babies while they were still married. She just couldn't find it in her heart to bring a child into this world under the circumstances and not knowing if her husband was going to try and work things out. She couldn't do to him what he had done to her because she was still in love with him at that point and wanted a baby from him. Kerry didn't want to make a baby with Tyrie, a man who would probably deny it or turn to walk out for a skinny chick. Kerry pulls out her diary and begin to unfold, after all that's what she have been doing for the past couple months.

Chapter One:

Into The Diary

Dear Diary,

Kerry's back at it once again, I thought this time it would be so different. Yes Jim accused me of cheating with Tyrie saying that he caught me cheating at the Jamaican club outside with a thousand people who knew her and her husband. All I was doing was hanging out with Tyrie because my husband and I were really cool with his brother, so we go to the Jamaican club because I knew that Jim family was having a party and when the party was over they all would come down the front street. So we out there chilling and getting ready to roll a blunt when I spot the police (writes Kerry in her diary) so I throw my arm around Tyrie neck to block the view of what we were doing with our backs to the approaching officer. I say to Tyrie

here hurry up and put this weed in the gar because I see the police walking this way. Kerry looks back again to see where the officer is at when she spots Jim walking her way, so she tells Tyrie here comes my husband and he ask oh where he at as he sits down on the concrete to finish rolling the blunt. Kerry responds while pointing in his direction oh he right there! Jim walks up and as Kerry tries to say something to him he keeps walking straight up to Tyrie and say, fuck nigga what are you doing with my wife? You do know she's a married woman? So as Kerry and Tyrie tries to explain what had just happened Jim goes off the deep end and tell Kerry oh you think it's a game, my cousin got that fie in the car right now. Kerry gets pissed and say did you just threaten me with a gun Jim, as his cousin is telling him fuck that hoe lets go cousin. So Kerry wave to the officer that was walking around and tell him as she pointing to the car that Jim was getting into, that they had just threaten her with a gun.

Kerry and Tyrie then leave and go their separate ways after finally smoking the blunt.

The next day Jim keeps calling her saying that he got another woman and how she a real woman because she has a job and a car. Jim also says he caught Kerry cheating over and over again, so Kerry gets fed up and say Jim you didn't catch me doing nothing but rolling a gar but since you accuse me of sleeping with him like you just walked up to the Jamaican club with my legs in the air, I am going to sleep with him since you keep on accusing me.

That is just what Kerry goes and does just that, sleep with Tyrie and now they are talking because Jim has a new girlfriend.

Chapter Two:

Tyrie

Dear Diary,

Kerry goes to pick up Tyrie because he had gotten
put out of where he was living and she took him to
Lehigh where she was staying at the time and
things were ok for a while until one day Kerry
decides to pick up his phone and go through it.
That's when she discovered that Tyrie would be
texting other girls when she would go visit her
mom, telling they that the house he was staying at
was his and inviting them over. Kerry began to text
them back saying hello my name is Kerry and I see
that you and Tyrie are supposed to be talking but I
am his girlfriend and this is not his house, he is
living with me because he got put out and have to
where to go, so when he text you again you can
tell him you know all about me. Also another thing

you would not have wanted to be in my house when I came home because I would've killed you and him, not because you knew of me but when you walk into this house you know that this is a woman set up and not a man and he don't pay no bills here to be inviting another woman in this home thank you have a great day. Kerry goes and throw the phone at Tyrie and say bitch you got some nerve if you ever in your life bring a hoe in this damn house I'll fucking kill you and bitch ass nigga stop telling these hoes this is your house cause bitch you don't own shit around here nigga. But what you can do is pack your shit and I will take you back to Clewiston and let your ass live on the streets like you were doing before I brought your ass here. So Tyrie gets mad man why the fuck you going through my phone and Kerry respond because I fucking wanted to nigga that's why and I knew you was up to some bullshit.

Chapter Three:

Kerry

Dear Diary,

Damn man I left a bad situation to get into a worse situation thinking the grass was going to be greener on the other side when in reality it is just about the same as I was going through if not worse. I wonder if I would've stayed with my husband Jim would things have gotten better or worse. Then again I knew I couldn't have stayed because he made it clear he didn't love me anymore and that he's gotten a baby on the way how can I go about being with a man whose made a child on me. Tyrie is not being a man of his word and I am wondering what else he is hiding because I know that there is much more.

Just as Kerry gets into writing more of her diary here comes Tyrie talking about bae listen it is something I need to tell you.

Kerry turns around and says: Tyrie what do you possibly have to tell me now?

Tyrie replies: listen bae it's this girl who I was talking to whom I never met but she used to send me her money, until she told me that she was H.I.V positive so my brother and I roasted her ass on Facebook and it ended badly because I was trying to tell her I couldn't be with her, even though I respect the fact that she told me she was sick I still can't be in a relationship with her.

Kerry Responds and say so you are trying to tell me that you was dating a girl who told you she was H.I.V positive but you never met her and she was giving you her money, but you never met her? That sound stupid to me, but what are you trying to get at what do I need to know about this girl?

Tyrie says well she got in touch with me on Facebook and I was trying to get her to send me some money, but she wanted to sit and talk all on the phone, so I told her listen I got a ole lady and if you not trying to send me the money then I am not going to be sitting on no phone with you because I can just go talk to my ole lady for that... Then she went to talking shit about you and say she is going to send you a message on Facebook, I told her that you weren't friendly and that she didn't want to come fucking with you.

Kerry says wait Tyrie so you telling me that whatever you and the sick chick got going on didn't go her way now she wants to come for me when I didn't send for her? Well pull you phone out and I am going to message her.

The Conversation

Kerry writes hello this is Tyrie girlfriend and from my understanding you wanted to speak to me, there is no need to message me when you can talk to me right now.

Channy responds: yes I wanted to talk to you and let you know that your man is trying to get me to send him some money.

Kerry: okay and he already told me that what the problem is because I don't have anything to do with your situation. So why do you need to speak to me again?

Channy: Well Tyrie and I were posed to be dating and I didn't know that he had a girlfriend.

Kerry: You the girl with H.I.V right? You did tell him that you was sick, so what makes you think that after you told him you was sick that he would be trying to go out with you didn't you learn from the shit you went through with him and his brother that the man don't want you, he was using you for your money baby girl.

Channy: First of all bitch he wasn't using me and he was going to come see me but he never got the chance to. Yes I told him I was sick because it's only right for him to know but he didn't have to act like that and now he with you fuck the both of y'all tell him I am not sending him shit.

Kerry: Pussy ass hoe I don't know who you calling a bitch first of all and secondly don't get mad with me because you thought that after you told a man you was sick he don't want you bitch. Then on top of that after you sent him money you actually thought he was still going to come and see you, how stupid are you girl. Listen this is between you and him I could care less if you are not sending him not money then you deflee need not be talking to me cause this not my issue now you have a good day goodbye!

Kerry says here Tyrie get your phone leave me out that shit, but I will tell you this; if you are still talking to that girl and trying to get her money then you need to quit fucking with me because you know the girl sick and you shouldn't even be entertaining the situation at all now get the fuck out my face I am done talking to your stupid ass.

Chapter Four:

The Party Drama

Dear Diary,

Tyrie and I goes over to his brother ex girlfriend house, who happen to be from Clewiston that I know very well name Dannie. Dannie is throwing a party and things are going well until she began to acting crazy and Kerry begins to snap. Tyrie gets mad and say man Kerry you tripping for nothing. So Kerry says: hell no I do not have time for this stupid shit I can always go home, because I didn't ask to come over here for this bull shit! I have already called my cousin Money and he is on his way to pick me up right now as we speak.

Tyrie: Well I am not going I am staying here.

Kerry: the only reason you want to stay is because it is going to be females over here, you must think I am stupid.

Tyrie then calls Kerry a bitch and all hell broke out, they begin to fight, so Dannie jumps into the fight and Kerry thought they was trying to fight her so Kerry is now fighting everyone when her cousin Money pulls up and Jumps out the car because he thought they was jumping on me.

Kerry gets home and leave Tyrie at Dannie house and while she's home playing around with her friends, there is this guy that's there and he says Kerry what you want let me put some money in your pocket. So Kerry and the guy are flirting around and go inside to Kerry bedroom. Just as Kerry is about to let the inner hoe come out she hear some banging on the front door, It's Tyrie with Dannie!

Kerry opens the door to let him in and Tyrie says where the nigga at that you was in here with bitch,

Kerry punches him in his face and says get all your shit and get out my house. I don't need you at all its nothing that you can do for me, you in a whole new city and you can't get any money. Bye as she throwing his shit out the door find you a way back to Clewiston and find you somewhere to stay.

Dannie says Kerry girl I thought I was crazy bitch you crazy as a motherfucker and will fight a man in a minute.

Kerry says first off I am not a bitch and secondly I don't give a fuck who it is or how many it is I'll fight anyone y'all better ask my husband shit he didn't make me soft he made me stronger and for this shit I am dealing with I could've just stayed with my husband.

Chapter Five:

My Cousin Jazzie

Dear Diary,

Kerry cousin Jazzie comes to stay a couple nights because Kerry is having so many problems with Tyrie and these women that he is talking to. Kerry went on to tell her cousin Jazzie about this girl she used to date name Tashie, and just so happens Jazzie know who she is talking about and gets in touch with her for Kerry. After Kerry and Tashie speak Kerry then tells Jazzie that she is going to take a shower so that they can go pick up Tashie when she's finished. Jazzie says cousin you do know you have your boyfriend over her and Kerry replies fuck that nigga I ain't got time for that shit this is my house if he don't like it he can leave.

Kerry goes in her room close the door and take a shower because her bathroom is in her room,

when she comes out she didn't know her cousin and her man would be laying in her bed, so she steps quickly back in her bathroom and say man y'all get out, what the hell y'all doing in here Jazzie I told you that I was going to take a shower. So after Kerry gets dressed she leaves with her cousin to goes to grab up Tashie! Once they return back that night was great it was like Tashie needed Kerry just as much as she needed her. So now Tyrie is walking around with a attitude and next thing you know he disappear and Kerry can't find her money and the rent man is coming soon for her to pay the little rent she owed him.

Kerry says ole hell no, who the fuck has my fucking money and I am so serious. She calls Tyrie and asks do you have my fucking money?

Tyrie Replies girl you sent your cousin to the store I ain't touched your money.

Kerry calls her cousin Money to ask him did he see Tyrie with any money and he says no, so Kerry says bring his ass here now cousin because one of these bitches got my fucking rent money.

So while waiting on Tyrie some kind a way a fight breaks out with Kerry, her cousin Jazzie and Jazzie boyfriend. Then after that fight was over Kerry and Tashie begin to fighting because of Tashie mouth. Soon as that fight was over here comes Kerry cousin with Tyrie and he is handing her money to her so Kerry grabs the money and then she swing on her cousin Money through the window and dive in the window on Tyrie to fight him. After all was said and done Kerry tells Jazzie to take Tashie home because nobody going to be talking sideways in her house. Tashie was like girl ill punch you in your mouth and Kerry swings on her, so now Jazzie is trying to get Tashie outside in her car when she calls Kerry a bitch an Kerry jumps in the window to fight Tashie. Once they got Kerry off Tashie, Jazzie hurried up and back the car up out of the yard. Jazzie returns a little later and Kerry tells her that her Uncle Nino has called and said that he is on his way back to her house for the night. Jazzie says well I am going to leave because you know he does not like me when he tried to talk to him and I told him no and that we are family. So Jazzie leaves but little did Kerry know that she took her rent receipt to Kerry mom and sister in Clewiston like she was going to get a ass whooping and also told them that Tashie told her Jerry was talking about her child being molested when none of that was true. On top of that she told Kerry mom that Kerry knew her and her boy friend was in the room when she came out the bathroom naked. Jazzie and Kerry had a big falling out, so Kerry called her mom to explain what really happened and that she never said anything about Jazzie baby. Kerry told her mom that Jazzie was out there arguing with Money and told him that he was the reason her child was molested and that everyone who lived on the street could tell her the same thing. Kerry then tells her mom I don't want Jazzie ugly ass boyfriend when I had Tashie and Tyrie over why would I want him, mom I told her I was going to take a shower in the bathroom in my room when I came out her and the dude was in my room. So Kerry mom says oh you were in your room they made it seem like you just came out naked. Kerry tells her mom that it was just a whole bunch of mess that she did not have time for.

Chapter Six:

The Beginning of the End

Dear Diary,

Kerry and Tyrie was having fights more and more regularly until one argument Tyrie takes it upon himself to steal Kerry computer with all her work and personal files on there, so Kerry called the police and pressed charges. Kerry ended up getting her things back and Tyrie was arrested but once again Kerry felt like hell I thought the grass was greener and I've gotten myself into this situation so I might as well stay. Tyrie was released from jail and for a short while things was okay between them until once again Kerry started catching him talking to other women. Kerry began to argue but let it go because she knew that the end of their time was coming soon. Kerry went with her mom to Lakeland fl and while she was there she applied for housekeeping at a motel. Once she returned home she received a call to be interviewed at the motel the next day so she had to rush right back up there. Kerry was interviewed and told that they would give her a call if she got the job so once again soon as she left and made it home, her phone rings and it's the manager saying could you come in tomorrow to start your three days of training. So now Kerry tells Tyrie I have a job in Lakeland and I'll be staying with my uncle and aunt until I get a place. So Tyrie thought everything was sweet, but Kerry had other plans. Her sister Tee ended up moving back to Clewiston and Tyrie decides to stay in the empty apartment because his people still didn't want him there at their house because he was rude and disrespectful.

Chapter Seven:

The Breakup

Dear Diary,

Kerry begins to write in her diary; I now know what I have to do, because I can't continue to be with this disrespectful ass man. Kerry calls Tyrie up and tells him that she sent his personal paper work to him along with 20 dollars and that she no longer wanted to be with him because she thought the grass was going to be greener when she left her husband after being accused of cheating with him, but things have been horrible so she could no longer be a part of that environment at all and they must now go their separate ways.

Tyrie was furious calling Kerry bitches and Hoes, so Kerry says see that's exactly why I can't continue to be with you because I already knew if you

would disrespect your mama like that then what would you say about me.

I am so sorry but I hope you find someone that can be with you and accept you for whom you are, I hope you get a job and get on your feet because the things I want and need you cannot give them to me. I have two children that need me and need a positive role model I messed up thinking that if I got with you the grass would be greener when in all reality I should've stayed where I was at and tried to make it work, have a great life bye bye and hung up the phone.

Conclusion:

Looking forward

Dear Diary,

After finally getting out of that relationship with Tyrie and trying to fix her life Kerry is working and began to start talking to this guy in prison who wanted to come to Florida when he got released from prison. Kerry was feeling this guy but when Brown Suga Festival came in her home town and she goes to the event little did she know that she would end up back with her first love, her baby daddy who broke her heart so bad. Kerry never in a million years dreamed that they paths would cross and she would be able to forgive him and be able to accept him back into her life. Love has its way of working and sometimes you cannot help who you love and even though I am feeling the guy from prison I have to be a woman and tell him what is going on and that I can't be with him no longer because my baby daddy and I was trying to make things work for the sake of our son. He told Kerry that he completely understood and respected her even more for being honest with him because every other girl he's had would've lied to him because he was locked up and if she ever was single again to reach out to him if she wanted to.

Dedicated To My Brother

In Loving Memory Of

Lorenzo Shelton Jr.

Second Half:

What Goes Around Comes Around:

Pay Back Is a Bitch

Written By: Lorenzo Shelton JR

What Goes Around Comes Around:

Pay Back Is A Bitch!

Hi I'm Larry and this is a story of how I fucked up. Now I know that you are thinking what kind of bull shit is he fixing to say and the guys are like is he stupid!

Well not all men deny when they are wrong so here we go sit back and relax you're going to love this.

February 15,2004 me as an 270lb dark skinned bowlegged well dress street Pharmacist living in Fort Myers Florida with my big sister Tina.

Well at this particular time it just so happen to be that my little sister Layla was over visiting for a little while, but my big sister Tina had a boyfriend named Moe, and he had a younger sister name Respusha!

Layla and Respusha were not that cool but they dealt with each other, only for Tina and Moe.

For number one: Respusha always liked me for herself, but she swallowed that somehow!

Then this one day I was standing outside my door handling my business when Respusha and her friend I had never seen before named Pickle come walking around the corner of the building and Respusha asked do you know where is my brother?

I then answered inside, in bed he just got in from work they kept him longer than usual.

She replies ok,

Then her friend started whispering in her ear and Respusha turns to me and says my girl want to know, Are you a Ju boy?

I answered half (why?)

She answered me and said pickle said you know what they say about bowlegged Ju boys.

I laughed and said you're a trip.

To be continued...............

Are you ready for this it's coming soon!

Written By:

Lorenzo Shelton Jr.

A Word from the Author,

I would like to thank you for taking the time out to purchase and read this book. I thank you and really hope you all enjoyed it as much as I did writing it.

I would like to give a shout out to my brother Lorenzo Shelton Jr. for taking the time out to write the piece that he did get a chance to write. Unfortunately he will not be able to finish it because he passed away 10/8/2017 and was laid to rest 10/14/2017, I really miss him so much.

He was my support system no matter what path I wanted to endure in life, he always had my back and I truly appreciate everything he has ever done for me and I would not have asked for it any other way.

Until we meet again big brother I want you to Rest In Love and Peace!

I Love You Always Your Baby Sister Lakyshia!

Also be on the lookout for my next book called: My Guardian Angel: Minister Lorenzo Shelton Jr. Thank you all again for taking the time out to read my work and I promise to keep them coming to you sooner than later.

God Bless you all,

Lakyshia Shelton

More books from the Author,

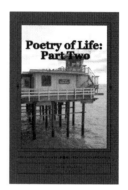

Purchase Links:

Www.createspace.com/8677332

Www.createspace.com/4522344

Www.createspace.com/4697383

Www.createspace.com/4697278

Www.createspace.com/4876336

Www.createspace.com/4707402

Www.createspace.com/6004221

Www.createspace.com/6014053

Www.createspace.com/4402848

Www.createspace.com/8544635

www.createspace.com/8332120

Email:

Author.Shelton28@gmail.com

Websites:
WWW.LakyshiaLShelton.godaddysites.com

WWW.Shelton1256604.site123.me/

LinkedIn:
www.linkedin.com/in/lakyshia-shelton-412796167

Facebook:
WWW.Facebook.Com/Author.28Shelton

Instagram:
WWW.Instagram.com/Author_l.shelton

Reviews on books:

www.createspace.com/Preview/1245687

www.createspace.com/Preview/1245688

www.createspace.com/Preview/1245689

www.createspace.com/Preview/1245690

www.createspace.com/Preview/1245691

www.createspace.com/Preview/1245692

www.createspace.com/Preview/1245725

www.createspace.com/Preview/1245726

www.createspace.com/Preview/1245728

www.createspace.com/Preview/1246594

www.createspace.com/Preview/1246654

Write To:

Lakyshia L Shelton

P.O Box 843

Clewiston Florida 33440

Made in the USA
Columbia, SC
27 February 2024

31958667R00028